WARCRY
THE ART OF INTERCESSION

TAMESHIA BLAKELY

WARCRY
The Art of Intercession

Copyright © 2024 by Tameshia Blakely
All Rights Reserved.
Printed in the United States of America

ISBN: 9798867924805
Imprint: Independently published
South Bend, Indiana

Subject Heading: PRAYER \ CHRISTIAN LIFE \ LITERATURE

This book may not be reproduced, transmitted, or stored in whole or in part by any means, including graphic, electronic, or mechanical without the express written consent of the publisher except in the case of brief quotations embodied in critical articles and reviews.

Unless otherwise stated, Scripture is taken from the King James Version, (KJV), which is public domain.

BIO

All praises to the Highest. My name is Tameshia Blakely. I was born on October 31, 1982, in Gary, Ind. I am the oldest of three girls, born to the proud parents of Burnie & Mischell Sanders.

I was raised in a very traditional household where both of my parents were very much a part of my upbringing. My father had accepted the call to the Gospel, I believe before I was even thought of, lol. Therefore, our entire household followed suit. However, at 40 years old I am elated that my father never came down, off the wall.

There was a standard of holiness that was instilled in us and expected to be maintained. To this day, that standard has kept me looking unto Jesus, the author and finisher of my faith.

Much to my surprise, at the time, I had the honor of experiencing many tests and trials. All of which has helped me develop a love for prayer and intercession. In the last 20 years, I have gotten to know the Lord like never before. He has been my shield and protector, my healer, and my friend.

I remember a specific time when I desperately needed to hear from God. I was in a very uncompromising position. I recall saying, "Lord this time you have to do it. I cannot do this one alone." As I laid my head down to sleep, I began to dream. In the dream I saw myself praying and teaching others how to effectively pray. I woke up in tears, hollering, "THANK YOU JESUS." I was excited about what the Lord had shown me. I was excited about what was to come. After which, I no longer wondered what my purpose was in ministry. I was convinced that my assignment was to teach others how to pray with passion and boldness, strategically, effectively, and fervently.

As you began this journal, I declare that you will experience God in a very real, and personal way; in a way that is unexplainable but only attainable in the spirit. It will be an experience that you will never forget, and it will shape your prayer life like never before.

I pray that your heart is ready to receive all that God has for you in this season and seasons to come. God is about to do something unexplainable in our prayer lives we will begin to see answered prayers. Upon writing this book, I was very hesitant. I was actually trying to complete this without telling my story. But, In many ways, God has confirmed that in order for readers to understand the outcome, at least pieces of the story must be revealed. So, I pray that as you read, you too will recollect the instances in your life that brought you closer to the throne. My hope is that you will be inspired to rekindle the fire and renew your fervency in prayer.

INTRO

As a child, having to remember bible verses, I used to wonder, how would I be able to use these scriptures when I got older. Because honestly, most of the people around me seemed to live for Christ out of obligation instead of willingness and desire. So, it would appear to most that their prayers were not being answered. I would sometimes ask questions like, why do we even pray? And when does God even answer our prayers? Why does His people suffer so much if they are truly living for God? Is it God's will for you to suffer? And If He loves us so much, why, why, why?

Once I had gotten to a certain age, I realized that GOD DOES HEAR THOSE WHO BELIEVE WHEN THEY PRAY. I learned that there must not be any doubt. Matthew 21:22 states, "And all things, whatsoever ye shall ask in prayer, believing, ye shall receive." In this particular passage of scripture, Jesus was teaching the power of faith in prayer. He used the fig tree as an example. Jesus had entered the city and the bible states that he was hungry. He saw a fig tree alongside the road and went to pick a fig from it but there were no figs on the tree. At which point he cursed the fig tree, stating that it would never bear fruit again. Immediately the tree dried up and died. His followers were amazed at how the tree dried up so quickly and they began to question. Jesus answered, if you have faith and DO NOT DOUBT, you will be able to do that and more. IF WE ONLY BELIEVE, GOD WILL MANIFEST ANYTHING THAT WE ASK FOR, THROUGH PRAYER!

Now, believing is more than just saying you believe. There must be a lifestyle that exemplifies total confidence in the power of God and His ability to be whatever you need Him to be for you in that very moment.

As you journey through this prayer journal, I beseech you to change your mindset and your approach to prayer. Prayer unlocks doors, breaks chains and breaths life, IF YOU ONLY BELIEVE WHAT YOU PRAY FOR AND IN THE GOD THAT YOU PRAY TO!

Isaiah 55:10-11 states, "For as the rain cometh down, and the snow from heaven, and returneth not thither, but watereth the earth, and maketh it brings forth and bud, that it may give seed to the sower, and bread to the eater;

VS.11 So shall my word be that goeth forth out of my mouth: it shall not return unto me void, but it shall accomplish that which I please, and it shall prosper in the thing whereto I sent it."

In my journey, I have learned that praying the word of God will be the only thing that unlocks doors, breaks chains, and breaths life. God's word cannot return to Him void. Therefore, He is careful to keep his promises to His children. Praying the word of God will ALWAYS produce results.

This prayer journal will walk you through some key bible passages, while teaching you how to target your prayers to receive effectual breakthroughs. So many times, we prayer and not incorporate the word of God. And if we do indeed desire for our prayers to be answered, we must challenge ourselves to know more of the word of God.

As I have researched and studied the word of God, I have adopted the ACTS (Adoration, Confession, Thanksgiving, Supplication) method of prayer. It is said to be first mentioned in a serial story by Marion Harland in August of 1883. I have found this to be most effective when implementing an effective prayer life. Like anything else in life, growth takes time and consistency. In fact, building an effective prayer life will be the most rewarding investment.

With the passion to pray and intercede, the most rewarding feeling is when God hears and answers your plea. That is more than money can buy. So, I admonish you to begin to study and read the word of

God as it will be your foundation to intercessory prayer.

How Prayer Changed My Life

Ever since I could remember, I have been going to prayer services, morning prayer, midnight prayer, noonday prayer, etc. I found out at an early age what prayer can do. As a kid my father had been having 6am prayer sessions. Man, it was hard to wake up, especially when I did not go to bed on time. But I had better press my way!

As a teenager, I experienced one of my first encounters with God during prayer. I had been sexually molested from the ages of 13-15 years old. Not knowing how to deal with this or who to talk to, prayer got me through one of the toughest times of my life. Early on in the situation, I did not hear a lot of positivity being spoken over my life. I know, I know what you are thinking, "But your family was……, You daddy is……., you go to ……. church. None of that means nothing if they do not or never have encountered anything like this so close to home and did not know how to properly help someone overcome. Whew, I know I just said a whole lot, but the truth is the truth.

Note: The ultimate goal is to help someone else overcome, just as I did. And I cannot do that by telling, printing pages full of cover ups or better yet, lies. Doing that will not help you and it definitely will not benefit me at all.

Now, where was I? Oh, I was molested from the ages of 13-15 and raped at the age of fifteen. As a result of that rape, I gave birth to a beautifully, purposed baby boy. However, this journey was not easy to go through. I began to pray to God like never before. I prayed so until I forgave all of those involved. It was in prayer that I forgave the family members that spoke ill of me and my destiny. I forgave those who intentionally sought to ruin me with their words. I forgave the ones that did not believe me, even the ones that knew and did nothing to help. I even forgave…. hold on to your seats…. I even forgave the ones that did it. DON'T TELL ME WHAT PRAYER CAN'T DO!

PRAYER SAVED MY LIFE, AND THE LIFE OF THOSE I ONCE HATED AND WANTED TO PHYSICALLY HARM (WHEW)!

It was then that I learned that prayer could not just be something I did when in need, it had to be a lifestyle. Prayer became my lifeline.

As I struggled to cope with all that came with being molested, raped, while in puberty (whew), my relationship with God grew stronger and stronger. I learned the voice of the Lord for myself. Previously, I had never really sought him for myself. I obeyed according to what, "my daddy said, or momma said." But baby, once I heard him for myself, I held on to it and wanted more.

There were times when I lost myself, I did not know who I was. At times I even questioned my purpose/destiny. But it was those 6am prayer sessions that kept me grounded. When you have a call on your life the enemy will try its hardest to make you confused of your identity. The devil will make you wonder if you have really been called or not. You will even, at times, doubt His call on your life because you are blinded by all of the hell and attacks that you have endured. But I am a living witness that even in the toughest of times, God is still, yet faithful.

I remember lying in the bed one night after I had just broken the news to my parents. I needed someone to hold me. I needed a hug and to be loved. I recall trying to get up out of my bed and it seemed as if my entire body was paralyzed. I tried to scream for help, but my lips were sealed shut. I immediately began to feel anxiety, that anxiety and fear became a blanket that covered every inch of my body from the inside out. In that moment, yes, I knew to call on Jesus, but I did not. I had become bound by fear, anxiety, rejection, hate, bitterness and much more. I had grown weary, in this situation. I did not have anyone around me to help me combat this in the spirit realm.

As I laid there night after night, before I'd shut my eyes, I would say to myself, "this time I'm gone call on Jesus." And night after night, repeatedly, the enemy would win, battle after battle.

Defeat had gotten the best of me, and it seemed as if there was no victory in sight. Some way, somehow, I had to figure this thing out, my sanity was slipping away, and I was quickly running out of faces to put on for the people. I was told that I had to be strong, because I had two younger sisters looking at me and they really had no clue what I was going through. They said, "we have a reputation to uphold, your grandaddy is the Bishop." They said, "our last name is _____, and we don't go through stuff like this." Man, the pressure was real. I had to decide whether it was better for me to help keep appearances, find more faces to put on or find a quiet place to talk to God and finally decide to keep my sanity.

Well for a while I chose to keep up appearances and find more faces to put on for the people. But God had a ram in the bush. And honestly, at first, I thought it was the worst decision. But it turned out to be the best thing that ever happened to me.

Before my baby boy was born, my dad had been relocated to Terre Haute, Ind., a city dead in the middle of nowhere. A city where we knew no one, and no one knew us. This was the worst decision yet, so I thought.

However, in the middle of nowhere is where I learned to hear God for myself. I learned to distinguish Gods voice, from my father's voice. I learned to trust God even when I could not see, hear, nor feel Him. And I learned that no matter what I faced, He was always there.

These spiritual lessons got me though and kept me grounded. Little did I know my faith would be tested again, in the same way. But this time, through prayer, my faith was stronger, and I knew the pitfalls that would be waiting for me on the road to recovery.

The Greater the Trial, The Greater the Victory

I had gotten the strength to move out and finally live on my own. It was through prayer that I overcame fear, at least to the point where I could be alone. I was doing my best to trust God and just live. But that enemy is cunning, when he sees that he is losing his grip he will use anything and anyone available to tighten that grip. And he did just that.

I can recall sitting on my couch one night. I heard a knock at the door. But since it was dark, and I was not expecting any company, I did not answer the door. However, right outside my window, I heard a man ask my neighbors if I was home. Shortly after, I heard a big boom in my son's room.

I said to myself, "I'm not picking up that radio tonight." He slept wild at that time and was always knocking down his stereo. So, I continued to prepare my bible lesson for chapel the next day. The next thing I know, there was a man standing two feet away from me. Dressed in a black hoodie, and pointing what seemed like a gun, at me. That big boom was not the stereo falling, it was someone breaking into my home. And when I looked up, I was at gun point. He forced me into the room next to my son. And as you could already imagine, he raped me. "Not again," I thought. In that moment, I remember praying to God, Lord please keep my mind this time, (I remember that like it was yesterday) because I barely made it through the last time. On the other hand, I remember thinking, "you do have a knife at the head of the bed, use it." But the way I was positioned, I could not take the chance of being shot and my son not having a mom. So, I laid there, crying, trying to hold on to what I knew I had prayed for. The man began to talk to me, trying to make me feel good about violating me. But every word he spoke pierced through like a knife stabbing me in my face.

Afterwards he forced me into the tub and turn on the hot shower water, trying to wash away all evidence. I was then made to sit on the couch until he had left. As soon as I could see that he was gone I quickly gathered some clothes, grabbed my son, ran to my car, and drove to my mom's house.

Upon arriving at my mother's house, I fell into my younger sisters' arms. At that moment I can remember my son, praying for me. He had to have been about 4/5 years old at that time. But he began praying, "Lord, touch my momma, she needs you now God, etc." That alone gave me strength and reminded me that God was still God. And that He would never leave me nor forsake me.

The devil is so strategic in his attacks. He literally studies our every move. Then he devises a very strategic plan designed to take us out. But my experiences have taught me that I have to be even more strategic, fervent and vigilant in my prayer life.

Later on, I found out that this man had been watching my every move. He had studied, PREYED on me even. He was very meticulous in his attack. This experience alone taught me to be even more strategic in our prayers and intercession.

This story may not be your story but whatever your story is, I pray that it has caused your prayer life to ascend to another dimension. Maintaining a fervent prayer life is vital in this walk as an intercessor. If our prayer life remains fervent, the enemy's attack will not be the very thing that hinders us. We might have to regroup but through prayer, we will remain unstoppable.

As a result of my story, I began to study how to effectively pray and see things manifest due to my prayers. And my prayer is that you too will be inspired to pray until things change!

What I have learned is that prayer gives you intel that goes far beyond what the natural eye can see.

It is through prayer that I continue to learn just how to defeat the enemy that seeks to destroy me. And when trials come my way, I am continuously armored and ready for battle.

I plan to spend this life teaching and empowering God's people to begin or maintain an effective prayer life. This alone will cause an uproar in the spirit realm, while sending a clear message of defeat to an already defeat foe, the devil.
Prayer has become my weapon of choice. And I plan to spend as much time as possible developing an army of prayer warriors. There is strength in numbers. Join me as we combat a mutual enemy.

WE FIGHT DIFFERENT!!

NOW, LETS GET TO WORK!

ADORATION: AABBA FATHER

When you pray you should always begin and end by praying to the Father, in the name of Jesus.

John 16:23-24

_____
_____
_____
_____
_____
_____
_____
_____
_____

You cannot approach the Father without also recognizing His only begotten Son!

John 14:6-7

_____
_____
_____

John14:13

ADORATION

Now, Adoration is simply giving God praise and worship for who he is. This part of your prayer should consist of words of praise and adoration unto the Most, High God.

It is nothing like being buttered up. Even though, as parents when our children come to us and they lead with, mommy/daddy you are so very handsome, you are the best, etc. By this time, before they ever get out the request, we most times have already made up in our minds to either grant it or deny it. It is no different with God. He loves to hear His praises from His children that He loves unconditionally and gave His only son for.

Psalms 100:4 states:

_____
_____
_____
_____
_____
_____
_____
_____
_____
_____

Adoration reminds you just who God has been and forever will be. It also makes you even more aware just how dependent we are on his power!

PERSONALITY OF GOD

Secondly, there are many distinct aspects of God. Therefore, when you pray, because God is ever present, it is important to know the specific names of God. This will grant you access and release Him in that specific area of your life. Knowing the names of God will reveal the very nature of who God really is.

Let us start by listing and defining just a few of the names of God.

Yahweh

_____
_____
_____
_____
_____
_____
_____

Jehovah Meqaddishkem

_____
_____
_____
_____

_____

Jehovah Nissi

_____
_____
_____

Jehovah Sabaoth

_____
_____
_____

Jehovah Jireh

_____
_____
_____

Jehovah Rapha

_____
_____
_____.

Jehovah Shalom

_____

Jehovah Tsidkenu

Jehovah Rohi

Jehovah Shammah

Adonai

El Shaddai

_____
_____
_____.

El Gibhor

_____
_____
_____.

El Elohim

_____
_____
_____

El Ro

_____
_____
_____
_____

El Elyon

_____
_____
_____
_____.

El Olam

_____
_____
_____

Now that we have given adoration and acknowledged who we are praying to, confess and ask for forgiveness.

PARDONING

It is imperative that we come boldly to the throne with clean hands and a pure heart.

It is nothing like asking your parents for something while hiding valuable information, fostering a fear of never getting a YES. Additionally, pride is the obstacle that gets in the way of us receiving that very thing that God so desires to give you. He is just waiting for you to confess and ask him for forgiveness, turning from your ways and allowing

God to abundantly bless you with your inheritance (what is rightfully yours).

Psalm 24:4-6

_____
_____
_____
_____
_____
_____
_____
_____
_____
_____
_____
_____

Forgiveness puts us back in right standing with God. It also makes us the best candidates to receive the Lord's blessings. And unbelievably, as my Apostle would say, He wants to bless us more than we want to be blessed.

ALL PRAISE BE TO OUR MOST GRACIOUS GOD!!

FORGIVE TO BE FORGIVEN

The way to be forgiven is to forgive. It is not ideal to boldly ask for something that we are not willing to give ourselves. Therefore, the only avenue that God provides for us to receive forgiveness is for us to forgive our sister/brother. Simple right, one would like to believe so.

The thing is this flesh of ours really wants to hold that grudge and not let go. Flesh really wants to be heard and not give an ear to hear. It really wants to be loved without the accountability to love. The flesh is actually no tricky thing, it is the enemy of God. It wants what it wants with no compromise. The flesh is at war with God.

It is to be sacrificed and consecrated, therefore, it wants ALL of you to be in bondage. Forgiveness is one way to remain in the bondage that the flesh desperately seeks for you to live in.

Forgiveness is so that you may enter into heaven. It secures your seat. Forgiveness is for your liberty. Yes, it may also help to free your sister/brother. But it is oh, most liberating to the spirit of God that lives inside of you.

Forgiveness is your ticket. It is for your peace of mind.

FORGIVE TO BE FORGIVEN!

Matthew 6:14-15

_____
_____
_____
_____
_____
_____

Ephesians 4:31-32

_____
_____
_____
_____
_____

Forgive constantly.

Luke 17:3-4

_____
_____
_____
_____
_____
_____
_____
_____

Matthew 18:21-22

After asking The Lord to forgive you, thankfulness is always in order. A thankful heart positions us to receive the abundant blessings of God.

Again, as a parent, when my child is appreciative of my kind acts, it makes me want to do more and even greater.
Thanking God reminds us of what he has already done while reassuring us that he can do that and more repeatedly and again…….

Thankfulness glorifies God.

James 1:16-17-18

_____
_____
_____
_____
_____
____.

Thankfulness brings peace.

Philippians 4:6-7

_____
_____
_____
_____
_____
_____

IN EVERYTHING, GIVE THANKS, AND RECEIVE UNDENIABLE PEACE!

Ok, after we have given God praise, worship, confessed our faults and repented, gave thanks, (whew) it is time to intercede. Now the initial steps are vital and are very intricate parts of the formula for effective prayer and intercession. This formula must not be taken for granted or omitted. It must not be taken away from nor added to. There are no substitutes. This is the formula for effective prayer and intercession. Now, let us intercede!

SUPPLICATION

WARNING: DO NOT PRAY AMISS!

When we pray IT IS IMPORTANT that we do not pray amiss. This is how the enemy will keep you bound.
What does it mean to pray amiss?
When you start or end a prayer without thanking & adoring God, you are praying amiss.

Philippians 4:6

_____
_____
_____
_____
_____
_____.

Colossians 4:2

_____
_____
_____
_____
_____

Whenever you pray and do not incorporate scriptural backing, you are praying amiss. The Bible is the most valuable resource for understanding the heart and mind of the Father.

Praying the word of God releases Him to SPECIFICALLY MANIFEST in your life.

John 15:7-8

John 15:4

Whenever you pray with fear over faith, you are praying amiss.

Matthew 2:22

_____
_____
_____
_____
_____

_____.

Hebrew 11:6

_____
_____
_____
_____

_____.

Anytime you pray for yourself more than you do others, you are praying amiss.
Job 42:10

_____
_____
_____
_____
_____

_____.

If your prayer only consist of begging God for your needs or desires, you are praying amiss!
If you refuse to set our pride to the side, confess our faults and repent, you are praying amiss!
If your will is not in alignment with His will, you are praying amiss!

Again, if your prayer is not laced with the word of God, you are praying amiss!

You get the point,

WARNING: THE FORMULA FOR AN UNANSWERED PRAYER IS TO PRAY AMISS!

Praying amiss makes us a target for demonic opposition. If we want our prayers to be answered, our intercession to be attended to, we must cross our T's and dot all I's. This makes it hard to impossible for the enemy to oppose our supplications made before God.

During supplication, the enemy is lurking for the smallest thing that he can use to block, delay, and or interfere with your answered prayer. Therefore, we must now study our enemy just as he does us. He is so very cunning in how he gets us off track and blocks the answers that we seek.

It is time to journey down one of the most intricate pieces of the formula......

UNDERSTANDING DEMONIC OF OPPOSITION

Ephesians 6:12

For we wrestle not against flesh and blood, but against principalities, against power, against the rulers of the darkness of this world, against spiritual wickedness in high places.

Now let us break this scripture down.

For we wrestle: It must first be assumed that there will always be a battle between the spirit and evil works.

Not against Flesh and Blood: The battle is not physical but spiritual. There is no material weapon strong enough to help you when a battle of this magnitude is at hand. The enemy of believers are not people or material things. The enemy that we face is indeed sin.

But against principalities against power, against the rulers of the darkness of this world, against spiritual wickedness in high places: The next thing that the believer must know is that there are ranks within the demonic realm/armies.

RULERS:
_____
_____
_____

AUTHORITIES:
_____
_____
_____
_____
_____
_____

POWERS:
_____
_____
_____
_____
_____
_____

PRINCIPALITIES:
_____
_____
_____
_____
_____
_____

IT IS IMPERATIVE THAT WE AS BELIEVERS REMAIN PREPARED TO EFFECTIVELY REBUKE THESE DEMONICE FORCES WITH POWER. WE CAN DO THIS BY PUTTING ON THE WHOLE ARMOR OF GOD.

One must never assume that on any given day, the devil has taken a break, HE IS ALWAYS ON THE OFFENSE. Lying and waiting to devour. Lurking in the dark places. Hiding in plain sight, in atmospheres you never thought he would be able hide in. He just cannot wait until you let your guard down. He walketh about seeking whom he may devour.

It is important to know who your enemy is, his plan and how he plans to execute it. The only way to know this, is to read the word of God and allow Great Jehovah to reveal it to you. He will not leave you ignorant of the enemies' devices. He will always show you. However, when he shows you, your spiritual eyes have to be opened to discern what the natural eye may not be able to perceive.

The enemy comes in many forms, open your spiritual eyes and God will show you.

Now, we have been given a formula that will cause the devil to flee.

James 4:7

_____
_____
_____
_____
_____
_____

Knowing who lives within us reassures us of the Great One!

1 John 4:4

_____
_____
_____
_____
_____.

The weapon may form but it will not prosper:

Isaiah 54:17

_____
_____
_____
_____
_____
_____

_____

Prepare yourself to fight…EFFETIVELY!

_____
_____
_____
_____
_____
_____
_____
_____
_____
_____
_____
_____
_____
_____
_____.

LASTLY, IT IS VERY IMPORTANT THAT WE AS BELIEVERS HAVE CONFIDENT IN THE FACT THAT WE WILL ALWAYS WIN!

ROMANS 3:37

_____

_____
_____
_____.

1 CORINTHIANS 15:57
_____
_____
_____
_____.

2 THESSALONIANS 3:3
_____
_____
_____
_____

REMEMBER, WE ALWAYS WIN!

HIS WORD + HIS WILL = RESULTS

Now that you have had a chance to research and learn about the most important and key elements for prayer, let us begin to formulate breakthrough prayers that will be effective in your daily lives.

A prayer is only effective if it coincides with the will of God and the word of God. Jesus taught his disciples how to preach, teach and PRAY!

Therefore, when going to God in prayer we must first understand that He is patiently waiting to answer your prayer.

The Bible is packed with effective prayers that ensure a breakthrough in every area of your life. Our only job is to hide the word of God in our hearts and speak it with our mouths. This will determine just how effective your prayers will be.

I have been graced with the unique ability to bring life to any dead or indifferent situation through the power of prayer. I am commissioned to bring back the reverence God through the power of prayer.

I pray that as you process through your prayer journey, you are inspired to continue and formulate prayers specific to your own life's circumstances. Prayers that will be effectual not only in your life but in the lives of those around and or are connected to you.

I have provided scriptures specific to various life situations that will inspire you to not only hide the word of God in your hearts but also to begin to declare and decree with governmental authority in the earth.

SCRIPTURES ON HEALING

Jeremiah 17:4

James 5:14-15

Exodus 23:25

Isaiah 53:4-5

Jeremiah 30:17

PRAYER OF HEALING

Using the scripture provided +, formulate your prayer of healing.

SCRIPTURES ON PEACE

John 16:33

Psalm 4:8

_____

_____

_____

_____

Isaiah 32:17

_____

_____

_____

_____

Philippians 4:6-7

_____

_____

_____

_____

_____

_____

2 Thessalonians 3:16

_____

_____

_____

PRAYER OF PEACE

SCRIPTURES OF DELIVERANCE

2 Chronicles 20:17

Joel 2:32

Luke 4:18

Psalms 32:7-8

2 Corinthians 10:3-5

Psalms 34:7

PRAYER OF DELIVERANCE

PRAYER OF FINANCIAL BREAKTHROUGH

Father God, in the name of Jesus. You are Jehovah Jireh, the Lord who provides. Just as you provided the ram in the bush in the place of Isaac.

Genesis 22:14

Adoration (insert)

_____
_____
_____
_____
_____
_____
_____
_____
_____

First and for most I pray for forgiveness and any and all disobedience in all areas of financial accountability. I stand now asking for wisdom over finances. I ask for forgiveness for any and all dishonorable giving and I decree and declare that the chains of poverty be broken and reversed Immediately. Thank you because I know that you have already given me what I need and more.

You are Jehovah Jireh who shall supply all of my needs according to his riches in glory by Christ Jesus. And we know that you are the creator, and your resources are limitless, and we have full access to your limitless supply.

God, I thank you because according to Philippians 4:6-7, I do not have to worry about anything, I have told us to play about everything. Telling you what we need, then thanking you for all that you have done. Only then will we experience your peace that exceeds all understanding and that keeps our hearts and minds as we commit ourselves to you.

Father, we dedicate our lives to you and the needs of your people. We desire to have unexplainable peace. God, we trust you.

According to Jeremiah 17:7-8, blessed are those who trust in the Lord and have made the Lord their hope and confidence. They are like trees planted along a riverbank, with roots that reach deep into the water, such trees are not bothered by the heat or wounded by long months of drought. Their leaves stay green, and they never stop producing fruit.

I decree and declare that I have full confidence in Jehovah Jireh and your ability to provide.

I decree and declare that all of my needs are met. Because I have gained access to your limitless resources.

I thank you because you have consumed all of my financial worries and have given us peace that exceeds my understanding.
I decree and declare that according to Psalms 115:14, The Lord increases me more; me and my children.

I declare that I no longer see things through a poverty mindset but that I now see through the eyes of financial freedom and total confidence and faith in Jehovah Jireh.

I thank you that my needs and wants are met according to Psalms 23.

I decree and declare that my little will become much and wealth and riches are in my house.

Now God, you said whatever we bind on earth shall be bound in heaven and whatever we lose on earth shall be loosed on heaven. According to your words, I bind generational curses and strongholds that seek to keep me in a state of poverty.

THROUGH THE POWER OF THIS PRAYER, I

USHER MY FAMILY INTO ITS WEALTHY PLACE!

PRAYER AGAINST DEMONIC OPPOSITION

Father in the name of Jesus, you are El Shaddai, God Almighty and you are El Roi, A God who sees.

Adoration (insert)

_____
_____
_____
_____
_____
_____
_____
_____
_____

Confession (insert)

_____
_____
_____
_____
_____
_____
_____
_____
_____
_____

He died on the cross for me that I might be free from sin and ALL demonic influence.

Thanksgiving (insert)

_____
_____
_____
_____
_____
_____
_____

Lord, I know that you are not a man that should lie, and your word is a sure foundation. Your words are the only real thing that I have to stand on and I know that you will cause me to overcome.

Lord, you said in your word….

According to Isaiah 54:17, No weapon that is formed against thee shall prosper; and every tongue that shall rise against thee in judgment thou shalt condemn. This is the heritage of the servants of the Lord, and their righteousness is of me, saith the Lord.

We decree and declare that the very weapon that was formed be dismantled in Jesus Name. I know that the devil is going to do his job. However, I have the power to rebuke, evict and dismantle every attack that you have planned for my life.

According to Ephesians 6:12, For we wrestle not against flesh and blood, but against principalities against power, against the rulers of the darkness of this world, against spiritual wickedness in high places.

I decree and I declare that I from this day forward, I will put on the strength of God and the power of His might. I clothe myself with the armor of God that I may be able to withstand Satan's attack.

According to Luke 6:27-29, But I say unto you which hear, love your enemies, do good to them which hate you, Bless them curse you, and pray for them which despitefully use you. And unto them that smiteth thee on the one cheek offer also the other; and him that taketh away thy cloak, forbid not to take thy coat also.

According to Psalms 34:7, The angel of the Lord encamped round about them that fear him, and delivereth them.

I employ the angels of the Lord to encamp round me and cover me with His wings of protection.

According to Proverbs 18:21, Death and life are in the power of the tongue: and they that love it shall eat the fruit thereof.

I declare and decree that Life and Death are in my tongue. I speak death to any and all witchcraft and curses spoken over my life and those directly connected to me.

And I declare recovery and restoration in my life, and the life of my family, over my business and every future business venture. I declare recovery and restoration in my ministry and those spiritually connected to me.

According to 1 John 4:4, Ye are of God, little children, and have overcome them; because greater is he that is in you, than he that in in the world.

I decree and declare that I will walk in more than a conquer anointing. For I am more than a conqueror. The devil will get no glory out of my life or those connected to me.

I cast down all fear that may arise. For fear is not of God. My love is made perfect and perfect love casts out all fear. I will not be tormented by the devil neither will I be afraid. The love of God covers me in every decision-making process, endeavor, in every situation and circumstance.

I hereby denounce all demonic opposition that may arise as I seek to do the Lord's will and carry out His plan for my life. Lord guides my footsteps and lights my pathway as I continue to serve you. Lord allow your word to rest, rule, and abide in my heart from this day forth.

IN JESUS NAME

SO, IT IS WRITTEN, SO LET IT BE DONE!

I pray that as you have journeyed through The Art of Intercession, you have gained a newfound passion for prayer and intercession. I decree the blessing of Deuteronomy 28:8 over your life. May the spirit of abundance compass you about that it shall overflow, that your cup runneth over just as God has intended for His people to live.

Made in the USA
Columbia, SC
08 March 2024